The Truth
About Technology
For
Very Small Business

GARY PAUL BRYANT

DEDICATION

This book is dedicated to honest small business owners everywhere.

CONTENTS

FOREWORD

I was honored when Gary asked me to write the foreword for this book. Gary and I have known each other for 20 years, first starting our relationship when, as director of market research for a leading market research company in Palo Alto, California, I hired him as a research analyst. We were pioneers in the telework movement, never sharing an office, but always working remotely using the technology available at the time. After that, we continued working together on various technology-related projects, both of us running our own independent small businesses, and both of us learning the ins and outs of applying technology to help us grow our businesses. And, we did all of this long before "the cloud" and "mobile" became commonplace.

Having been involved in the technology market research space for more than 30 years and learning about the problems that business decision makers face, I appreciate the focus of this book – namely, helping small business owners to use technology more effectively. According to the US Census Bureau, small businesses with fewer than 20 employees provide more than one in six jobs in the United States and account for the vast majority of business entities. Very small businesses make up the bulk of these organizations, making them a critical component of the US economy. The right technology choices can help these businesses to become more efficient – and, the wrong choices can most definitely have the opposite effect.

From a technology perspective, there has never been a better time to be a small business owner than today. And, quite frankly, never a worse time. Technology choices abound, particularly those available in the cloud, to help small business operators manage every aspect of their business. These include email communications, accounting, file sharing, social media, mobile messaging, supporting remote workers, conducting online meetings, maintaining a Web presence, managing leads, and a host of other capabilities. At the same time, however, small business owners are inundated with so many options – and there so many IT consultants willing to "help" them – that many business owners simply don't know where to begin. These owners often get oversold a package of services that are designed to help them grow and manage their business, but often end up causing frustration more than anything else.

So, what should small business owners do? First, as discussed in this book, it's important for them to get educated about their options and avail themselves of the many good sources that are offered for free or at low cost. Very small business owners can learn how to solve problems with a minimal investment in time even if he or she is not a "techie" and don't have a lot of time to devote to technology education.

You don't always have to use an IT consultant to solve your technology problems – you can take ownership of your business and find good solutions on your own. Solve problems one step at a time, focusing on solutions to your most pressing problems first rather than developing a "technology master plan" that will solve all of your problems at once.

Finally, understand that small business owners can learn about the technology they need in small chunks, solving point problems along the way, without having to resort to "experts" that might cost lots of money and might not solve their problems.

I sincerely hope that you enjoy this book and take its lessons to heart – they will be worth your time and effort!

Michael D. Osterman
President
Osterman Research, Inc.
Black Diamond, WA

1

WHAT CAN A TECHNOLOGY BLOVIATOR
DO FOR YOU?

You've heard them at conferences; you've read their techno-babble infused pontifications on hundreds of technology websites. You're afraid you might throw yourself into a vat of melting cellphone touchscreens if you have to listen to one more technology bloviator talk about the sea change of paradigm shifts in the upcoming confluence of scalable management decision-making objectives concerning enterprise exchanges and IT infrastructure implementations.

The problem for the non-technical business owner is that, in their attempts to impress you with their knowledge-base of web-enabled minutia, there is usually a grain of truth at the base of their self-important presentation. That grain of truth is this: somewhere, somehow, your business needs to address its technology infrastructure. But what is that exactly? Even small businesses can no longer ignore the role of cloud-based computing and the secure low-cost collaboration and productivity tools. It's still a challenge to understand what is the best technology for very small business. Simply put, the best technology is *appropriate technology*.

That means using simple tools rather than enterprise grade IT monsters that suck out all f your profits while you and your staff struggle to understand what they do.

In a survey conducted in 2014 by Osterman Research of mid-sized and large organizations collected between June 6 and June 9 of 2014, respondents show an increasing use of cloud-based productivity tools by end-users.

* 11.0% of end users are on Office 365, growing to 24.3% by mid-2016
* 5.9% of end users are on Google Apps, growing to 9.4% by mid-2016
* 1.3% of end users are on BPOS/hosted Exchange, growing to 2.8% by mid-2016
* 0.7% of end users are on IBM SmartCloud, growing to 1.5% by mid-2016

That's just Microsoft; Google Apps is growing up, lesser known players like Zoho and ThinkFree are also offering lower cost cloud-based solutions for smaller businesses. And for very small business these offerings can be cheap or even free.

So before you dismiss the next technology conference as a complete snore, there might be some take away from very small business, search out the balance of appropriate technology that solves some business problems at a level you actually can understand and implement. While the language of technology can sometimes be a bit monotonic, the presentation just a bit unimaginative, the advantages of cloud technology is tremendous. Small business owners might want to step out of their comfort zone long enough to consider the use of appropriate technology in their enterprise.

2

THE 30 MINUTE DOWN-TIME CATASTROPHE

Mission critical applications, disaster recovery recommendations, risk assessments and recovery plans; you've heard the words, you've read the warnings, and so you choose to table the discussion until a later date. As a business person, you're focused on the bigger picture. Furthermore, your company hasn't experienced any significant downtime since you've been running the company. I've never been in a fatal car wreck either.

Whether your business operates on a single Hewlett Packard computer running Windows XP, or you can proudly point to three hundred workstations located at multiple sites, the reality is You are driving your enterprise. You should fasten your seat belt and pay attention to the road ahead.

Recently, you might have read about Microsoft's Outlook server outage in the news, but do you recall Facebook's downtime on June 19th or Verizon's 90-minute power outage back in April? According to WCAX News in Burlington, Vermont, computer systems at

Vermont's largest hospital went down in June of 2014 and employees were forced to enter information on paper. Stuff happens.

Ironically, in the 2014 Small Business Survey conducted by Brother International Corporation in partnership with SCORE, 72 percent of small business owners thought that technology would be a better return on investment rather than new employees. Sixty-three percent of respondents admitted they were overwhelmed by the number of technologies available to help them run their business.

So here we are, on the one hand, we can see that threats to the business enterprise are real and in fact, do happen. On the other, decision makers are overwhelmed by technology strategies that might help alleviate the problem. Neither over-thinking your IT issues to the point of making a non-decision, nor proceeding as if your morning bowl of Lucky Charms will keep the company safe, are realistic options. New productivity apps provide some benefits that mitigate the expense and embarrassment of an IT meltdown.

Once you've migrated your IT to the cloud, for example, time-consuming migrations and backups are a thing of the past. Power failure is no longer an issue. Everyone in the company automatically uses the most recent version of the software. Video conferencing is a reality for customers and employees. Hardware failures are now only less costly annoyances.

Imagine that you get a call from your top salespersons that his laptop is frying because he left it on the car dash in the sun. He has three weeks' worth of contact and sales info on it, creating a disaster of catastrophic proportions.

With a Cloud-based productivity tool set as your company's cranial engine, the salesperson can simply head over to a Best Buy or some other computer store, pick up a replacement laptop or tablet and be up and running in 30 minutes- with no loss of data! In a pinch, the salesperson could have accomplished the same thing with his smartphone; a much more productive outcome than heading back to the office and starting from scratch.

New business, fresh growth initiatives, new employees can and do have a big impact on IT infrastructure- even to the point of breakdown. Cloud-based solutions even for very small business, goes a long way to resolving that issue.

3

EVEN VERY SMALL BUSINESS NEEDS TO PAY ATTENTION TO BIG WORDS

Regulated environments can be a time-consuming and expensive headache for businesses. Not only do companies have to create and adhere to their own internal sets of policies and procedures, but most businesses are also required by federal and state laws to comply with specific standards of operation, i.e., regulatory compliance.

Before you wonder what that has to do with you and your business, consider the problem of the Orange and Alexandria Railroad in Virginia during the Civil War. Dozens of railroads across the South, most serving only a small geographic area, taking local cotton to seaports for trade, operating exclusively in their own territories.

When the Civil War broke out, and railroads were pressed into military service, a surprising discovery was made. Troop and supply trains simply could not travel from Biloxi to Raleigh; each state had their own track gauge. If two adjoining states didn't have the same track width, a train had to stop. All of the cargo and passengers were unloaded from one train and reloaded on to an entirely different train because one operators' trains couldn't fit on another's tracks. This lack of planning is regarded as one of the major contributors to the loss of the Civil War for the South.

The same problem started to come up for businesses in the 20th century, different pipe sizes, different paper thickness, problems arose in nearly every part of the trade community. That's when the International Organization of Standards (ISO) came into existence. Soon after came the development and rapid expansion of the Internet, causing best practice standards to be developed by individual businesses and industries, as well as state and national governments. As a result, some agreements, guidelines, and laws have been implemented in an attempt to bring order to an ever-growing business community.

Today there are numerous agencies, both public and private that provide standards for various business operations. Here's just a few:

HIPAA

The Health Insurance Portability and Accountability Act (HIPAA) exists to provide a standard for the protection of electronic health information. Any business that is involved with medical records and patient information is required to comply with HIPAA. Microsoft's Office 365 has built-in features that assist with HIPAA compliance.

FISMA

The Federal Information Security Management Act of 2002 or FISMA was enacted to address information security issues regarding all federal agencies. If your organization does business with the federal government, you may want to make yourself familiar with this law.

ISO 27001

Headquartered in Geneva, The International Organization for Standardization or ISO is an international voluntary organization that develops commercial, proprietary and industrial standards. ISO 27001 is the ISO security standard that was published in 2013.

FERPA

Simply put, The Family Educational Rights and Privacy Act (FERPA) is a law that protects student information. The law applies to any school that receives federal funds.

GLBA

The Gramm–Leach–Bliley Act (GLBA) is in place to guide financial institutions. The law requires banks and other financial institutions to safeguard any consumer information they might collect and provide easily accessible information regarding their privacy practices.

Conclusion

These are just a few of the regulatory requirements your business might be subject. At the time of this writing, Microsoft, with its' Office 365 for Business, has gone to great lengths to make regulatory compliance easier. Microsoft has also created the Office 365 Trust Center that explains its role and efforts in making Office 365 a secure and regulatory compliant business tool. One more low-cost tool for very small business.

4

SMALL CHANGES CAN YIELD BIG RESULTS
ONLY IF YOU ACT

Business owners often struggle with budget issues. In the Northwest, some businesses have the added challenge of dealing with severe seasonal changes in customer activity. Half of the year they are overburdened with work orders and no time to 'run' the business, while the other half of the year they sit quietly at their desk twirling a pencil, no customers and cashless, wondering how they could ever grow their business out of this conundrum.

A local contractor came to my home the other day for a small plumbing job, like many other experiences I've had with contractors, he was late for the appointment, and, in fact, was filling in for someone else who was suddenly put on a different job.

"We're swamped!" he said. "Sorry, we didn't get back to you, but I haven't had a day off in three weeks."

"Sounds like you have a pretty successful business, are you that busy all year?" I asked.

"Heck no! I'll be lucky to get five customers from October to March. I should probably advertise, but I just don't have the money."

So there it is, the most common complaints by small business people; no time to give attention to the back office, no money to grow the business. The truth is, many small business owners are too busy driving their company into the ground rather than learning, testing, and investing in what works. Complaining about their current familiar predicament is much more comfortable than initiating a change. The good news is there are solutions. Here are just a few things you can do to keep yourself from wrecking your business.

Loosen Your Grip

Sooner or later you're going to have to trust someone else to run your business. You might not want to admit it, but other people are capable of doing much of your job. Believe it or not, there are probably a few good people around you who are worthy of your trust. Mentor them, give them responsibility. You might be surprised at what respected employees can accomplish, and it will only help your business thrive.

Give Up the No-brainers

Why on Earth do you still have a land line? Why are you paying for premium print cartridges? In fact, if you're not writing a sales letter, put your printer in draft mode and save even more on expensive printer ink. Why stop there? Millions of companies have given up paper and hard copy altogether. Start emailing invoices to your clients and save the paper and postage costs. Set up PayPal or some other mechanism to let customers pay their bills. Become your own efficiency expert. Remove the barriers to sales!

Embrace Technology

You hate it; I get it. Now it's just one more thing you need to get over. You can't run a competitive business today without technology. Get a smartphone. Start checking your emails, respond to them at least twice a day. Find out what Twitter is, and LinkedIn. Learn how to text. There's a whole world of commerce going on all around you and if you don't have a clue, well then, you just don't.

If all of this seems daunting, consider getting help learning about new technologies that will give you more time. Remember this is your business and its 2016, not 1985. If you just can't bring yourself to making the smallest changes in your attitude about technology, then get rid of it all together. Get rid of your email address. There's no sense in giving potential customers the false hope that you're interested in their business. The same goes for that 10-year-old website. If you can't take it seriously, take it down. You just look silly.

PTFT

You can analyze things to death, but while you're doing that, your business is losing more market share, your company is losing competitive advantage. You continue to waste money on things that don't work, and you're losing the confidence of your employees. If this sounds depressing, maybe it's time to turn things around. PTFT. Pull The Friggin Trigger and act!

5

YOUR COMPANY SERVERS ARE IN THE CLOUD, BUT YOUR DATA MAY BE ON A PLANE TO BEIJING

Any responsible business owner needs to tread carefully when making technology infrastructure decisions, but over-analyzing the pop scare of the day (is my data safe in the cloud), may result in taking your eye off the ball. How much of your company is in the pockets and backpacks and briefcases of employees and heaven forbid, former employees?

Cyber security is big business. Spam, malware, viruses, phishing scams, you've heard the terms before, stories about them are in the news every day. Some companies including Microsoft, Amazon, and Google have invested heavily in cloud security.

Recently, Google announced a new initiative called Project Zero aimed at stamping out those evil code exploiters- those miscreants bent on finding software flaws that they can exploit for a variety of nefarious reasons. Indeed, Google has their own team of hackers that purposely seek out flaws in web software looking for the same vulnerabilities. The difference is that when they find these weaknesses, they alert the software company so they may apply a patch.

Microsoft, the creator of Internet Explorer and more recently Office 365 and the newly minted Windows 10, has brought an arsenal of security tools to the web including Microsoft Security Essentials and its support website Microsoft's Safety and Security Center. Consequently, for its cloud service Office365, Microsoft has established the Office365 Trust Center that describes in detail the built-in security features of Office365.

Not So Security

So you might be feeling pretty good knowing that Google is hunting down code glitches on the Web and Microsoft has armored your business by securing it with Office 365. Your servers may be in the Cloud, but your data may still be on a plane to Beijing.

While companies are obsessing about cloud security, the most likely problem might start at the same business address. Laptops, cell phones and tablets used by employees and contractors are often chock full of intellectual contraband, and your lack of policy enforcement might be to blame.

A recent study from Symantec Corporation found that fifty-six percent of employees thought it was ok to take competitors' trade secrets (a week ago that employee might have been working for you)! Another sixty-two percent of employees indicated that it was ok to take employer documents home to work on them, but didn't see any problem with leaving those documents on their personal machines once the work is done. Only thirty-two percent of respondents said their managers viewed data protection as a priority. Yikes.

Guarding the Front Gate and the Back Door

How many employees do you have? How many cell phones do they all have? How many company laptops are in the home offices and kitchens of your current and former employees? How many employees are using their personal tablet for work? How many keys and passcodes are floating around? Do you even know? Add it up: That's how many potential real world data leaks you have. That doesn't even include someone breaking into your company offices and data centers.

By all means, move your office to the cloud. Take advantage of cross-platform apps, productivity tools and cloud security measures. Make sure your antivirus and malware programs are up-to-date. Just don't lose focus on the real world, where you and your business thrive, where your employees work, where your efforts are born.

6

DO YOU NEED A COLLABORATION TOOL?

A typical day, a typical office, the receptionist is logging incoming calls, greeting customers and checking on the whereabouts of salespeople in the field. The accountant is in the back office, accounting. Your tech guy is hunched over his computer as usual; you're not even sure how he occupies his time. You hear the phone ring, and you learn that the receptionist is speaking to a key client. Before you can take a bite out of your raspberry scone, your receptionist storms into your office and informs you that a major project is about to unravel. The client hasn't received the artwork from creative, and their board of directors is calling a meeting in two hours. They want the presentation today. Your sales lead for this client is currently on a plane to San Diego, and your outsourced creative department is 'outsourced' for the day.

This scenario (or one very much like it) plays out all across the globe, but they all don't end in a state of panic or dread. If your business is using Microsoft's Office 365, Google Docs, or even DropBox or Asana, all of which include a number a collaboration tools to remedy situations like the one described above.

When Features Become Benefits

In Microsoft's case, for example, in addition to the usual Office365 productivity suite of Word, Excel, PowerPoint and Access, Microsoft also includes a number of tools focused on collaborative technologies. These include business class email, instant messaging (IM), video conferencing, real-time screen sharing, real-time note-taking, document sharing via SharePoint, chat and shared calendars. Also, all of these features are available for desktop computers, laptops, tablets and cell phones. While all of this is very impressive, they're of no benefit until you make use of them. So the real question you need to throw around the office is, what kind of benefit can you get from them?

Many of us might be familiar with Microsoft's Skype or Microsoft Instant Messenger, but you may not have heard of Lync. Lync Online, part of the Office365 for Business environment, takes these earlier collaboration tools to the enterprise with a distinctly robust feature set. Lync's feature set allow employees and customers (who have installed Office 365 for Business) the ability to employ video and chat communication strategies; all through a secured Microsoft Lync server. Should you care with only five employees that see each other at lunch every day?

When Benefits Become Advantages

Deploying the full Office 365 suite of Business Premium real-time tools which includes Outlook, Lync, OneNote, and SharePoint, along with the Office 365 productivity tools of Access, Publisher, PowerPoint, Word and Excel, your business may realize significant cost savings, depending on your company's configuration and practices. Microsoft's experience in deploying real-world solutions to millions of small and large businesses worldwide, as well as its impressive investment in continuing to develop new cloud-based technologies, promises to provide a competitive advantage to any business willing to make the choice. All of these enterprise solutions are touted in one digital mag after another. It wouldn't hurt to educate yourself about these issues, primarily so you ascertain whether they can really save you money or not.

7

YOUR BUSINESS IS A MOVING TARGET: THE CASE FOR BENCHMARKS

We all like to see progress. For a business, increased sales revenue, new product launches, new employees and even new furniture can all create the appearance of progress. The real question is this: Is the business healthy?

Benchmarking has been around for a long time. It's simply the process of comparison. Companies like to use benchmarks when comparing themselves to other companies. A sales or marketing professional might proudly exclaim; "This month Zany Big Spiral Widgets Corporation just lost three large clients while we increased our Spiral Widgets accounts by six!"

That might sound like a benchmark, but it isn't. If Zany Big Spiral Widgets started the month with one-hundred accounts and our business only had a total of twelve, there's not much point in making that comparison.

Effective benchmarking can produce actionable results if you take the time to benchmark your company against itself. To do this, you'll want to take a snapshot of your business processes now and again at a future date, say in one to three months. Something like an efficiency assessment, benchmarking your enterprise will highlight the impact of your policies and procedures and how they affect your day-to-day business processes, including sales and marketing efforts, employee productivity, customer service quality, spending, and your company's technology services.

Using your company's computer and IT services as an example, make a list of routine processes that can be counted. This list could include not only your website traffic statistics but also your mail server log and phone log. There may be other 'events' that aren't included in your automated log so take some time to identify these. Where automated logs aren't possible, prepare a plan for employees to spend the month quantifying 'events' that might change their behavior. A few examples:

- How many times you receive a complaint about not receiving an emailed document?
- How many times did the server 'go down' this month?
- How many times were online meetings postponed due to technical difficulties?
- How many times did the discovery of a virus or malware result in a loss of productivity?
- How many times were incoming calls routed to an answering system, rather than being answered?
- How many callers hung up before leaving a message?

By monitoring this kind of activity, even for a few weeks, patterns of behavior and deficiencies in policies, practices, and infrastructure will emerge. As business owners, we're often preoccupied with counting receipts or dollars spent, meeting the day-to-day needs of our customers and staff, but there is an inherent cost to doing so inefficiently.

You may be losing potential new customers simply because your phone system is too complicated for callers. Your server might be clogged with malware, or is too old to meet your current business demands. When you started your business ten years ago, your phone company's internet connection seemed like a workable solution. It's quite possible that your business has outgrown its current provider, and a more robust and secure connection is required. Malware infested old servers, limited capacity of your local network or an Internet connection; all contribute to frustrated clients and employees resulting in lower productivity and ultimately lost revenue.

Gaining competitive advantage is essential to keeping your company in the black. Take the time to benchmark yourself. Get the answers, make decisions. It's what you do.

8

A HACKER COULD BRING YOUR ENTIRE BUSINESS
TO A SCREECHING HALT

So I recently came across two interesting small business studies. The first, the Small Business Technology Survey pointed to some encouraging trends in IT implementation as well as an overall eagerness and acceptance of new communication technologies. Survey participants revealed that they are using smartphones (74%), an increase of 17% from the last sampling.

Ninety-four percent of small business owners indicate that they are concerned about security issues. Indeed, they also admitted that many of them (44%) have been victims of cyber-attacks, resulting in considerable monetary damage. In fact, those respondents who had hacked financial accounts suffered an average loss of $6,927.50. Exacerbating this dilemma, business accounts do not fall under the consumer protection act. Furthermore, the SBA survey reports that 75% of respondents were unaware of this fact.

In the 2012 National Cybersecurity Alliance/Symantec National Small Business Study, 45% of survey takers reported that their businesses are very dependent on the Internet for daily operations. Yet 47% of respondents in this study thought that a data breach would have no impact on their business operations, 32% felt there would be a short-term impact and 11% had no idea! It's becoming very clear; a hacker could bring your business to a screeching halt, but so could you. Being in denial of the real dangers of operating a business in a connected world, remaining uninformed to your company's security holes and the remedies to mitigate the risk are more of a threat than an outside perpetrator. Not only is a disaster recovery plan essential, but even more so, a disaster-avoidance plan.

The C-Level Review

Gone are the days where you can relegate your IT policies strictly to your IT department. Security risks can be extremely damaging to the company as whole, and that should be the concern of every business leader at the highest level. If you don't have a disaster avoidance plan, start here.

Backup your data in the cloud and off, be sure you understand how to recover your company data so that your business can be operational in the shortest amount of time.

Keep all of your software current, hackers routinely exploit latent software; ask almost any rookie webmaster.

Make policy and make sure everyone follows it. Eighty percent of business owners in the NCSA survey say they don't have a security policy in place. Does your company allow employees to work from their own smartphones and tablets? What happens when one is lost or stolen?

Keep up on technology developments. Yes, there is a lot of noise out there in the digital media world, but it's not all noise. You need the latest information and the latest technologies to improve your business and protect its assets.

Your company's security and uninterrupted operation require a combination of creativity, innovation, and skilled implementation. Your employees and technical team are there to provide that implementation, so delegate to them what needs to be done. The creativity and innovation of your business, however, starts with you, so don't be so eager to delegate yourself.

9

THE SKY HAS FALLEN, AND XP MARKS THE SPOT

In the late 1990's I was working in a small Palo Alto IT consultancy that as it turned out, was making considerable revenue helping major corporations navigate the so-called Y2K dilemma. After all, the clock was counting down to the year 2000 and believe it or not, much of the software running the world's businesses seem to be lacking a piece of code that would allow for the recognition of any date beyond December 31, 1999. Apparently the number 2000 hadn't been invented yet. Thankfully, the doomsayers were a bit too aggressive, and after the noise ebbed and the dust settled, the world was pretty much unscathed.

Spring forward to last April of 2014 and much of the same bloviating rhetoric was rewritten, scraped and posted all over web media and beyond. What would latent and lazy businesses who haven't ever upgraded to a newer version of Windows do when support for XP finally stops? Would they capitulate and upgrade? Would they abandon technology altogether and return to the abacus, fountain pen, and rotary phone? Would the rest of us even care? Are all of the warnings valid? Will the sky fall on businesses that refuse to upgrade?

You can certainly get enough 'artificial intelligence' from semi-informed friends and coworkers that will infer answers to these questions. They'll tell you to get a good 3rd party antivirus program, make sure you have the last available version of XP installed and warn you about opening attachments on an XP machine. If you're adamant about maintaining XP indefinitely, it almost goes without saying that you'll simply need to disconnect from the Internet altogether, which will give your XP computer the comparative functionality of the historic Apple IIe.

And what about Microsoft? Are they sticking to their promise of no XP support? According to Catalin Cosoi of Bitdefender, it turns out that just a few weeks after walking away from XP, they issued a patch for an Internet Explorer zero-day vulnerability that turned into a permanent issue for XP users. Apparently Redmond is having a hard time breaking up with the world's two most famous consonants as well.

Several surveys put the worldwide use of XP anywhere between 18 and 25 percent of all Windows users, so there's no question that a significant, yet disparate horde of Windows fans loves hating Windows no matter how good it gets.

10

LEFT BEHIND ON THE ROAD AHEAD

Back in October of 1994, long before the Cloud, the smart phone, flat screen TV and the Oculus Rift, Bill Gates published his signature book, 'The Road Ahead' which outlined his vision for the future of technology in society. More than twenty years have passed, and while gargantuan changes have taken place in many segments of our new society, small towns, and very small businesses seem to have been left behind on the road ahead.

Some small business websites are still being created and managed by well-meaning nephews and nieces, and the accounting is done by Aunt Martha, who thinks QuickBooks will simply take too long to master. For others, a computer network is a group of well-connected people that share a single computer, not the other way around. So the question is: Is running a business in a small town still a disadvantage in the modern world of Internet, Wi-Fi and collaboration?

Some people choose to start their business in a small town because they simply live there. "We were born and raised here, both personally and as a company," explains Kyle Drone of Dinger Bats in Ridgway. In an interview with the Southern Business Journal recently, Mr. Drone added; "We have everything we need, and it's less expensive to do business here. Plus, we have the Internet and all of the shipping companies come through town every day. You can be in business any place in the world today."

So aside from the obvious reasons, of being native to an area, why would any company choose to move to a small town? Manufacturers may find the labor costs lower, and if you've tried to open a small business in a major city, you might find that regulatory compliance, taxes and the simple "cost of doing business" is just prohibitive.

Tom Welge, vice president of technical sales and general counsel for Gilster-Mary Lee in Southern Illinois, says, "Sometimes, if you're in a growth mode, finding enough of a workforce can be a challenge."

Still companies do it every day.

Sufficient Internet bandwidth and the technical support needed to run a larger business can sometimes be a challenge as well. The US Department of Agriculture provides some grants to rural communities to develop technology infrastructure as well as training resources to help build a viable business environment.

Have small towns been left behind on the road ahead? Not so much in Whatcom County, Washington, where some very well-known businesses continue to thrive, including Alsop, Intalco, British Petroleum, Botanical Labs, Barleans, DIS Corp, Totally Chocolate and Nature's Path, just to name a few.

As the world becomes smaller and our perception of local community expands, business competition also expands, becoming even more intense, and the need for even more innovation increases with it. As technology takes on a larger role in our daily business, local business owners, who may even be competitors, have an opportunity to explore news ways to work together, so both their community and their respective businesses thrive in the 21st century.

11

WHEN THE INNER CIRCLE GETS OUTDATED

You thought you were the smart one. The brother or sister that knew how to replace the family VCR with a TiVo. You read books about HTML and helped your uncle add a shopping cart to his locksmith website. You were in the know. Now it's twenty years later, and you run a business.

Fifteen years ago, you bought the company's first computer and helped set up its first network, when you bought the second computer, and attached a cable between the two. Now the company has 49 employees, 33 workstations, two websites, a whole boatload of phones you'd like to ditch altogether, and they tell you everything needs to be backed-up every day.

The Outside World

In the outside world you hear about one large corporation after another getting hacked; Target, Home Depot, even Facebook and Google have been violated! Someone just told you about how many healthcare records had been breached. You didn't want to hear that.

Internally, you've got customers complaining about computer downtime, employees complaining about everything running slow, and there have been new complaints about the software not being compatible with new client files. The two interns that run your website tell you that you need to be on Facebook, Twitter, Pinterest and Linked In. You've only heard of two of those. Your second hire, who now looks after your network, told you to move to the Cloud, while your daughter who worked in accounting during the summer, insists that your whole system is outdated. Ouch, and you were the smart one.

Just Enough to Be Dangerous

The old cliché, 'Knowledge is Power' is still true, no matter how overused the term is. The problem comes in when the possessor of said knowledge has accumulated precisely enough of it to satisfy himself of his new-found capabilities, but not quite enough to be of any use to you. Homemade IT departments in small companies all over the world suffer from this phenomenon. That is; you are forced to rely a person that has so far convinced you that they have sufficient skills and knowledge to solve your problem, when, in fact, they do not.

These are often well-intentioned employees and friends, people who may have demonstrated some technical aptitude at some point, are more than willing to volunteer for tech duty. After all, it's a secure position, and problem solvers get respect, we all want that. What they are lacking is the technical depth of understanding via certification and real business experience that tempers their technical skill with the ability to reach a successful conclusion that demonstrates a real benefit to the enterprise.

The homemade IT perspective will convince you to change the problem rather than solve your problem: "You don't need to install that, it will take months to get it online, and the cost will be outrageous. You'd be better off hiring a data entry person to simply type the info in."

If this strikes a chord, you know who you are. Chances are you just figured that the backend of your business could be worked out at a later date, because, at that moment when you hired the office supply store salespersons to be your IT department, sales were what mattered.

And of course, you could prove that to us if we could do a quick comparative analysis, but apparently your computers are down. One more reason online software services can be very cost-effective for very small business.

12

WHILE YOU WERE AWAY:
E-BOOKS, CRAIGSLIST, REGIN, AND GARTNER

While we're busy managing our businesses and juggling our customer, partner and personal obligations, technology continues to advance, detract, improve, and destroy our perception of our little chunk of responsibility. Here' are just a few things that happened while you were away.

E-books Sales Continue to Grow

You've owned a Kindle for years, what's the big deal? Well, PriceWaterhouseCooper renewed their prediction that E-books will outsell hard copy books by 2018. Right now, about 45% of all book sales are e-books. It was just a few years ago that an e-book was simply a text file you opened in Notepad and downloaded from Project Gutenberg.

For me, the proliferation of e-books and readers is more of a 'canary in a coal mine' kind of thing; it's an impressive reminder that the future almost always becomes the present, whether we like it or not. Remember that the next time someone conjures up something that looks a little silly, like an Oculus Rift.

Even Craigslist is Not Immune

The venerable, yet humble Craigslist website was disrupted last year for a few hours, redirecting unsuspecting visitors to other websites. While no malware was used to destroy data, nor was any personal information stolen, hackers were able to successfully gain access to the website's DNS server (the server that hosts the domain name pointers) and modify its parameters resulting in the disruption. So the good news here is, you can still safely hunt for new employees and used laptops on the cheap.

Just When You've Adjusted to the New Reality, Along Comes Regin

You've finally come to terms with the idea that your data may never be completely safe, and that you have accepted the fact you have to budget for network security going forward. While that's good news, it won't help you with Regin, a very complex surveillance malware that has been spying on businesses, governments and individuals since 2008.

So far, no one has been able to narrow down where this stealth software originated. Experts agree that it's very sophisticated and was probably created by a government, of which only a handful have the necessary skill level. You can thank Symantec for that discovery.

Gartner's 2014 CEO and Executive Survey

Gartner calls it a "Risks On" Attitude, but really, business leadership is continuing to grapple with the impact of technologies they don't fully understand. Digital marketing, E-Commerce, customer experience management, business analytics and the Cloud are the top areas of technology that responding CEOs have reported to Gartner. You can get your own copy of the report at the Gartner website for only $1295, or you can simply read the last sentence over again. Either way, it's a symptom that technology is outpacing our understanding of its impact.

So there you have it, a small sampling of the many events that can have a significant impact on our businesses and personal lives- or not. After all, you're the decision-maker, shouldn't you be making that choice?

13

SOMETIMES WE JUST NEED TO REFLECT ON JUST HOW COOL TECHLOGY CAN BE

I don't know about you, but every so often I just have to look around and consider how lucky I am to be working in a field where our imaginations can transform the real world. No matter what our specific function is in the economic world we live in, many of us are coming to realize that everything we do is deeply embedded in a complex technology infrastructure, impacting every aspect of our lives. Sometimes it can be a source of stress, at other times, it simply makes us smile.

Dissolvable Medical Machinery

Recently Google announced they were working on a pill chock-full of nanoparticles that, once absorbed into the bloodstream, targets different types of cancer to detect the disease in its earliest stages. Now, researchers at Tufts University have created an implantable medical device that stops bacterial infections with heat and then dissolves itself once the job is done. How cool is that?

Moving Mountains Without Moving

Millions of us take it for granted; that little predictive keystroke app, that suggests the most likely words we might use when we create our zillions of text messages on our smartphones and tablets. For some with limited dexterity and range of motion, it's the gateway to a world they wouldn't know otherwise.

Stephen Hawking, the world-famous cosmologist, stricken with Motor Neuron Disease for much of his adult life, has Intel and Swift Key to thank for a much-improved technology that allows him to communicate with the rest of the world.

Unable to move any of his limbs, Dr. Hawking relies on a cheek sensor that communicates with an infrared switch that helps him choose characters he wants to type. The new Intel system, Assistive Context Aware Toolkit, uses a custom software provided by Swift key to providing a much-improved experience.

It's good news for Stephen Hawking and the thousands of individuals and their families and friends affected by Motor Neuron Disease and Tetraplegia.

Expensive Toys for Regular Folks

The Carbon Flyer from Chris Hawker and Trident Designs is making personal drones fun again. Billed as the first all-carbon fiber drone, the Carbon Flyer appears to be fairly crash proof, and if you have a mind to test the theory, you'll have direct evidence via the onboard video camera.

Instead of wires, strings and old fashion radio, Trident Designs has chosen to incorporate Bluetooth control. The entire project is being crowdsourced on IndieGogo (another impressive example of tech-mob convergence) where you can invest in and receive one yourself for about ninety bucks. Like I said, how cool is that?

14

NOTHING CHANGES IF NOTHING CHANGES

The impression most people have of company CEOs, corporate presidents, and other business leaders, is that of the visionary, the person who 'knows' where the market is headed and ultimately where the company is moving; he or she is the far-sighted company luminary. Interestingly, if a person has the vision condition of farsightedness or Hyperopia, they can see far away just fine, but not all that much nearby.

Often, when a business is in crisis, the company leadership looks far and wide for causes and culprits, but sometimes, the root of the problem is in the building and sometimes in the mirror.

Best Asset, Worst Enemy

It may be perceived as low sales, a poor economy, bad advice or a host of other reasons as the cause of company dysfunction, but more often than not, it is simply an untrained staff, insufficient infrastructure, lack of oversight, poor process, or absent management.

All of it can bring a company to a state of paralysis; and all can be made worse or remedied, by the company leader. So how can you save your business?

Change the problem

So product sales are slow in coming, getting ready to ditch the high paid sales team? Sounds like a sure-fire way to make the company look profitable again, on the other hand, you wouldn't advise an obese person to lose weight by amputation, would you? The problem may be related to sales, or it may not. It could be that, while your flagship product might be brand spanking new and shiny, nobody wants the silly thing. Maybe the problem is, you never really thought to ask your customer base what they'd need -much less what they would be willing to buy.

Hunt for Problems

You might be known for being an unflinching optimist, but the fact is, your business exists because somebody else has problems. I hate to be the bearer of bad news, but your company has problems too. Don't take the word of any of your employees; that everything is peachy-keen or worse, hunky dory. You have problems. Your Internet connection sucks, your servers always crash, two people in your shipping department are months away from retirement and haven't put in a decent days' work since 2007. Find your company problems, find your customers' problems; become a hunter.

Provide the Tools. Really

How many of your employees have come knocking on your door, asking for a new spiral jig smacker or similar tool? The employee explains that the old jig smacker gets bogged down two or three times a day. The employee points out that they could be smacking four times as many jigs if you sucked up and got the new Jig Smack 400 XL with built in Jag Adjustors. You know how many times you smiled and said you'd look into it. It's your company for Pete's sake, so provide the tools your people need to get the job done.

Fix High Leverage Problems First

What's a high-leverage problem? It's any barrier to completing your mission statement. High leverage problems usually affect multiple departments at the same time, so they're easy to identify and sometimes can be fixed by simply installing a new piece of software. On the other hand, it might be expensive, like replacing the CEO.

High leverage problems can drain the motivation from your employees, sour the enthusiasm of your customer base and bring your productivity to a standstill. Whatever it is, be it a new IT network, new machinery, a simple pep-talk or a complete rewrite of policies and procedures, fix it. Otherwise, nothing changes, if nothing changes.

15

BOX, GOOGLE AND MICROSOFT:
A COLLABORATIVE REVIEW

For quite a while now, cloud-based software has become the go-to technology for both start-ups and large businesses alike. In fact, pen drives and portable hard disks are now considered to be cumbersome technologies, prone to getting lost and their data deleted, whereas cloud-based solutions allow users to access and manipulate files directly from their web browsers.

As crucial as these products are, not all of them are tailored towards each and every type of business. Some may offer only basic storage while others may provide a full suite of applications that are synchronized on and off of the cloud. While there are more than one hundred collaborative tools on the market today, let's take a look at a few of the most popular.

BOX

Box is an online storage service specifically built for collaboration. Its target audience is mostly professional users, but it also caters to ordinary consumers since it adopted the freemium model. Box focuses exclusively on cloud storage, so it does not have a desktop client that takes care of local backup.

The best thing about Box is its level of integration with other popular web apps. For example. Word documents can directly be created and edited from within Box's website. The service can easily be integrated with Google Apps as well. Box also works with NetSuite and Salesforce CRM. Users can share and retrieve files stored on Box from within Salesforce. The same goes for NetSuite.

Box also excels at reporting and auditing. It offers admin tools that allow full access to their enterprise's account according to IP address, date and time, email and username. Administrators can also track and keep tabs on individual files at the document level.

Google Apps and Office 365

Google Apps are built for companies where desktop integration is not the focus. Everything is in the cloud and for companies with little to no existing infrastructure or stringent organizational requirements, its ideal.

Office 365, on the other hand, is built for businesses who have to use productivity apps on a constant basis to run their business. Office365 is the cloud version of the industry standard, Microsoft, taking this productivity behemoth one step closer to complete business ubiquity.

Google Apps and Office 365 both offer trials, but their approaches vary. Getting started with Office 365's P1 Plan for small businesses is simple enough. The user can either use Microsoft's own domain and start the trial or add a customized domain name that will require ownership and verification before it can be used. Using your own domain is a bit tricky to setup and getting some help is recommended.

With Google Apps, however, the user must first go through domain ownership and verification before starting the trial.

Office 365 has the upper hand here simply because it works immediately with SharePoint, which is hugely customizable, albeit somewhat complicated to use. On the other hand, Google Docs, though easy and intuitive, is relatively limited regarding functionality, but this may not be an issue for a very small business.

Both Office 365 and Google Apps offer similar features, but there are stark differences between them. Let's start with Google Apps first.

With Google Apps, users get a free cloud-based email for a maximum of 10 users for as long as they use the service. They also get 25 GB of email storage and 1 GB of document storage. Google uses a free, non-industry standard file format and its editor (Google Docs) lacks rich document formatting. Google Docs, along with other apps, use the same UI elements, so customers who have been using Gmail or any other Google App, for that matter, will feel right at home. Microsoft's Outlook can also be integrated with Google Apps Sync.

Google excels at making cloud document sharing and collaboration simple out of the box unlike SharePoint, which has many more features but is also harder to set up. As mentioned before, Google Apps are mainly cloud-centric, so there's not much regarding offline access on there. Documents can be opened and edited, but that pales in comparison to what Microsoft offers with its Office suite of applications. Apart from that, Google also offers very basic IM through Google Talk.

With Microsoft Office365, business packages vary, but in one scenario, an account comes with free cloud-based email for a maximum of 25 users. Each user is given 25 GB's of email storage and 1TB of document storage.

Of course, Microsoft makes use of its docx format that is a huge advantage as they are perfectly compatible with Office applications. As for the UI, Office 365 uses the same ribbon interface that has been the staple in a lot of Microsoft's applications since it was introduced in Office 2007.

Microsoft's trump card here is SharePoint, which works out of the box with Office 365. Users can use its full set of features for file collaboration.

16

REALITY CHECK:
INSIDER THREATS AND YOUR BUSINESS

When it comes to threats to the integrity of core business operations and computer systems, most business owners and managers tend to focus the larger part of their attentions on those threats that come from without, like malicious hackers, economic spies and such. External focus isn't necessarily the only perspective. Threats to your enterprise can also come from within, and hackers don't necessarily care about your business size.

Not all company employees and contractors are above stealing secrets that they can then can sell or put to nefarious use. Indeed, one of the earliest cases of computer crime occurred during the years 1970 to 1972, long before the advent of the World Wide Web.

Albert, the likable, trustworthy, night shift computer operator of the National Farmers Union Service Corporation of Denver, turned out to be Albert, the Saboteur. After 56 consecutive hardware failures, all happening at night, company executives installed cameras to watch Albert on his shifts. It wasn't long before he was caught in the act. When asked his reason for causing such significant damage, it turned out that Albert was simply lonely, arriving when others left, leaving when others arrived. The computer repair crew summoned each night after his nightly act of sabotage was a welcome sight.

Human experience has proven, time and time again, that the greatest dangers to our security, in fact, come from within, from those in our immediate circle. Once you think about it, this makes perfect sense; these people know the company and its inner workings the best. They also know what and where the company's biggest weaknesses are.

Who's Keeping Track?

Since 2002, a group called the Insider Threat Study team, a branch of the CERT (Computer Emergency Response Team), a division of the Software Institute at Carnegie Mellon University, has worked with the Secret Service to "identify, assess and manage" potential dangers to data and critical systems as well as the other major vulnerabilities. They concentrate their studies on employees who overstep the bounds of their authorized access to the IT systems of the companies they work for, in a way that negatively affects their security and threatens their missions.

What Companies are Most Vulnerable?

Insider Threat Study has found that four types of companies are most likely to be the targets of insider threats: banks and other financial institutions, critical infrastructure companies, information technology and telecommunications companies, and government agencies. They have published works on each of these types from 2005 to 2012.

How Insider Threats are Typically Handled

For the most part, fully 85 percent of all insider intrusions have been handled internally, with legal action being taken in only 8.5 percent of these cases. Businesses have resorted to contacting law enforcement or filing a civil action in only 12 or 3 percent, respectively. The most common reason management has chosen to deal with the problem from an internal standpoint is that they could not identify the perpetrator, while others kept quiet for lack of enough evidence to prosecute. In either case, it belies one to think that the real reason companies are reluctant to speak out about network incursions is their embarrassment for not maintaining adequate security efforts. Additionally the process of reporting crime becomes public record, and significant exposure of proprietary company operations could result.

The Threat Landscape

Despite what we've said in the introduction, the latest statistics indicate that only 28 percent of all electronic crime events are known, or at least suspected to have been caused by insiders. The other 72 percent come from external sources. Of those that were most costly or damaging to the organization, however, the percentage of insider sources surges upwards of 46%, a trend that should be of concern to every business owner.

17

THE SONY HACK:
WILL SMALL BUSINESS FINALLY LISTEN

To say that the security breach at Sony two years ago was an IT catastrophe would be an understatement. A group of hackers known as the GOP or "Guardians of Peace," stealthily acquired most or all of the company's sensitive materials, from emails to user passwords and much more. The group, rumored to be affiliated with the North Korean government, launched the cyber-attack on Sony in an effort to prevent the company from releasing the movie, "The Interview," which fictionalized an American attempt to assassinate the Korean leader. Sony has since canceled their 2014 release, but thanks to a very public backlash, Sony has considered alternative ways to distribute the film.

However, the brazenness and successfulness of the attack is secondary to gaping holes in Sony's network security. Information gleaned from documents the hackers released to file-sharing networks highlighted the lax security implemented by Sony's IT department. For example, Sony employees, from the top echelons of the company down to the lowest ranking trainee were allowed to send passwords through unencrypted emails. Any experienced IT engineer will tell you that this is a vulnerability just waiting to be exploited.

It's not that there weren't any warnings to alert Sony that an attack like this was possible. In 2011, hackers launched an attack on the company's Play Station network in which the personal information of millions of customers was stolen. Even then, Sony execs were heavily criticized for not taking cyber security seriously. In fact, the company had laid off two IT security experts, just weeks before the breach.

Apparently Sony is not alone in the nonchalant attitude taken toward security by many businesses despite the overwhelming onslaught of network breaches. In 2013, retail giant Target was hit by hackers, and the result was the loss of sensitive information for 40 million debit and credit card holders. Not only did the event create a public relations nightmare, but banks had to take drastic measures, including putting limits on the dollar amount a customer could withdraw.

In September of 2014, home improvement giant, Home Depot confirmed a breach of its security and the loss of sensitive customer information. Cyber security experts say the Home Depot attack looked eerily similar to the Target attack. Credit card numbers and CIV codes were being sold on the same dumping site as the Target data. Some say the breach in security had been open for months.

Hackers originating out of China carried out a decade-long cyber-attack on communications giant Nortel. The hackers were able to breach security safeguards put in place by Nortel's IT department, by gaining access to just seven passwords. During those ten years, the hackers helped themselves to sensitive information like technical papers, emails, and research and development documents.

The devastating breach in Sony's cyber-security should be seen as a warning to other businesses to reassess their security protocols, disaster recovery plans and data encryption policies.

In the Sony case, not only did the hackers abscond with terabytes of sensitive data, the malware that they used to invade Sony's systems, also erased all of the original data, leaving the hard drives wiped clean.

Nobody said security would be easy—that's why bigger corporations have IT departments, and every other company struggles with budget allocations or stubbornly lives in denial that an attack will ever come their way. In any case, there are some steps all businesses can take that would go a long way in closing up some of the access points in a company's communications and security systems. Here are some of them:

- Increase security awareness training for employees. Training in this area will help eliminate simple worker mistakes, like opening suspicious emails that can contain viruses.

- Improve encryption technology so that mobile workers have password-protected laptops, encrypted Wi-Fi and similar measures in the event the device is stolen.

- Improve intrusion prevention on all critical systems that are linked to the Internet like servers, email systems, and other data storage devices by installing a firewall or better yet, installing a UTM (Unified Threat Management) System.

- Some breaches occur when a worker innocently visits another website. Blocking worker access to certain websites could avert a lot of "drive-by" attacks.

- Perform vulnerability scans on every system on the corporation's network on a regular basis.

- Regularly scan for system vulnerabilities and apply patches whenever one is discovered. Don't rely on Microsoft updates alone.

- Keep an eye on suspicious behavior, it may be worth your while to install an employee monitoring system.

- Theft accounts for a large amount of data loss. Make use of off-site backup systems or consider migrating your enterprise to the cloud. Never rely on a single layer backup system.

In any event, small and large businesses must be willing to ensure that their enterprise, their data, and the data of their customers, is protected. The cost of making security enhancements pales in comparison to the damage inflicted by a malware attack both real and perceived.

18

PLANNING ON BEING IN BUSINESS
5 YEARS FROM NOW? PLAN FOR CHANGE

The time is ripe for small business. New technologies come online all of the time, the success of small business ventures has never been more promising. Social networking has already provided companies with a low-cost, direct route to millions of potential customers. An opportunity exists for immediate growth and expansion from the moment a business owner decides to engage. While technology companies themselves feed off of the ever-increasing pace of transition, the rest of us struggle to keep up with last year's technical requirements. So before you pat yourself on the back for updating your email address, let's find out what's in store for business in the near future.

Cloud technology

If you're a large company, you're probably already in the cloud. If you're a tiny one-person operation, you're probably also in the cloud, due to the plethora of free cloud accounts available for the simplest of home office needs. If you're an average small business in the United States, with 10 to 100 employees, you might be reluctant to make the move. Cloud technology allows businesses, and individuals, to not only store important documents and files off-site but work with them in real-time from multiple locations on multiple devices.

You might have heard about the cost savings that comes as a result of moving your business to the cloud; this is probably not directly true. Anyone responsible for the daily operation of a business is not likely to put all of their faith (and data) on a remote server without some kind of assurance that it will still be there tomorrow. Hence even while companies move to the cloud, they often employ their local server as a backup utility. The real savings for users of cloud technology is higher productivity, less downtime and fast reaction time to fluctuating business circumstances. So if you're not working in the cloud, you soon will be if you want to stay competitive.

Microsoft Azure

Microsoft's Azure combines both IaaS (Infrastructure as a service) and PaaS (Platform as a Service) to create a network model that allows you to construct, deploy, and manage applications in a way that optimizes nearly complete control of your business's entire productivity spectrum.

Azure has eliminated the barrier that used to exist between public and private storage mediums. Azure's enterprise-proven hybrid cloud technology brings together the best of both worlds, making it possible for you to expand your business options with less reliance on a full-fledged IT department. Azure provides more flexibility concerning the applications your business may require to stay operational. Microsoft's Azure makes storing data, system backup, and recovery more efficient, regardless of which applications are deployed.

19

DOES BITCOIN HAVE A FUTURE IN LEGITIMATE BUSINESS?

Possibly, but don't hold your breath. The Consumer Financial Protection Bureau called it "The Wild West" of financial products. According to an article appearing on the Association of Corporate Counsel's website, Reuters writer Mary Grams lays out a detailed look at Bitcoin indicating that many governments are looking at the implications of BitCoin, but few have embraced it.

On the other hand, after some initial hesitation, more and more businesses are taking steps to modify their payment plans to include Bitcoin. Major corporations like Internet giant Amazon, Microsoft, and even some travel agencies are making the upgrade to accept Bitcoin.

Bitcoin is a virtual currency that is not regulated by a central bank. Its popularity arises from the fact it can be used for transactions anywhere in the world, and all transactions are discrete, secure, and untraceable. Depending on the industry your business operates in, you might find yourself playing catch-up in an e-commerce world looking for any way to break down the sales barriers of web business. Proceed with caution.

What Else Could Go Wrong?

It's a legitimate point of view if you find yourself overwhelmed by the vast array of technical innovation that has exploded around us. Not only the technologies and processes mentioned above but drones, 3D printing, advanced robotics for shipping, delivery, and driverless cars will all have a major impact on all aspects of our lives in the coming few years. Read some magazines, load up your Kindle or iPad, hire some professional guidance, and envision your business in the new future.

20

MICROSOFT'S FAVORITE COLOR IS AZURE, WILL IT BE YOURS?

As the evolution of the business world continues, the challenges associated with computing infrastructures are also evolving at a corresponding pace. Cloud computing has introduced exceptional solutions to some of the enigmatic issues associated with business management. However, cloud computing itself can create challenges and overload. This is where Microsoft wants you to think Azure comes in. Azure is a comprehensive cloud computing infrastructure (IaaS) and platform (PaaS) that is designed for the deployment and management of cloud services and applications via a global network of Microsoft-operated data centers.

Microsoft Azure offers a Windows Server-based computing environment that is designed to facilitate the persistent storage of unstructured and structured data, the management of cloud applications and asynchronous messaging. Another powerful advantage offered by Azure is its capacity to facilitate a comprehensive range of services, including connecting on-premises applications and users to cloud-hosted applications. Windows Azure Web Sites (WAWS) is one such example. Additionally, Azure can assist a business with authentication, implementing data management and other related features, such as caching.

Primary Benefits of Azure

There are many benefits associated with the use of Azure as a cloud storage and cloud computing management system. This platform is replete with the functionality to effectively manage challenges associated with cloud computing for businesses.

- Familiarity with Windows: Because Azure is Windows based, business IT professionals will be able to write applications using programming languages with which they have experience.

- Windows VMs: The applications that run on Azure run through virtual machines, meaning that each instance of an application will run on its own VM on a 64-bit Windows server operating system.

- Scalability and Flexibility: Azure allows a business to create applications that run on a highly reliable system while providing impressive scalability — with the capacity to scale from 10 to 10 million users — without the need for additional coding. According to Tom's IT Pro, NBC Sports was able to stream 17 days of the Olympic games to mobile devices via the web, reaching more than 100 million viewers across multiple regions.

- Development Tools: Visual Studio is not only one of the most popular development tools ever built, but it is also considered to be one of the best. Microsoft's own WebMatrix is a rapid website development application that dovetails with the Azure environment allowing for rock-solid deployment of websites, largely due to its built-in sandbox environment. A wide range of web development scenarios including ASP.Net, PHP, Node.js and Python can be deployed on Azure.

Some Potential Disadvantages

Generally speaking, the flexibility associated with Microsoft Azure and its functionality as a SaaS, PaaS, and IaaS significantly reduces any disadvantages that it may have. There is no need for a business to install their own operating system since the Azure platform provides the ability for programmers to write code in a variety of languages. It should be noted that support for third-party applications may not be included from Microsoft.

Rapid Growth

According to a Bloomberg report, Azure sales are experiencing exceptional growth as Microsoft Azure becomes a more formidable competitor with Amazon's cloud management platform. The report reveals that Azure has surpassed $1 billion in annual sales. Many experts see this growth as being indicative of the platform's evolution. The report reveals that the infrastructure market is the fastest growing aspect of the cloud market. It is projected that the market will grow by an estimated 38 percent annually to reach $30.6 billion in 2017, which is a significant increase when juxtaposed with $6.17 billion in 2013.

Azure for Governments

According to Government Technology, some state governments have deployed the Azure platform, including Alabama and Texas. Texas expanded its Criminal Justice Information Security Addendum to integrate Azure Government. At the same time, Alabama is deploying what is perceived as a hybrid initiative that involves Azure Government to facilitate the management of its entire Medicaid Health Information Exchange and CARES systems.

The migration of governments to Azure has significant implications. One thing that moving to the cloud does is reduce the cost for taxpayers by implementing a more efficient and cost-effective system. The system also meets all government security requirements, which means that highly sensitive structured data will be stored under a higher level of safety. There is a significant number of safety regulations that are implemented by the federal government, such as HIPAA and FedRAMP, etc. State governments are spending a substantial amount of money to ensure that they are meeting these regulations: however, Microsoft Azure Government deals with those regulations, so state governments don't have to.

Conclusion

To say that Azure is a comprehensive solution to every business enterprise would be foolish. For most very small businesses it's not cost effective, for others, there isn't a compelling need. What Microsoft has accomplished with Azure is both impressive and worth considering for any forward thinking organization with an expanding future.

21

WHEN YOU NEED TO LEARN IN A HURRY

Whether you're the new hire or a seasoned business owner, there are times when you need to brush up on critical business skills. While it's sometimes cost effective to simply outsource a task, recurring costs that accrued because you won't take 30 minutes to learn something new or relearn something old doesn't make sense. Luckily for you, there is a growing number of online resources for micro-training; skills that you can quickly pick up from online education portals. These sites provide a big range of tutorials, interactive learning tools and video instruction, all designed for rapid learning.

You should note that there is a big variation in both pricing and subjects covered. Some courses are free while others may have a membership fee or ala carte pre-payment for each course.

Lynda.com

With more than 3,000 courses and 260,000 tutorials available on video, this online learning portal offers a vast amount of technology training, covering different types of office software, systems, and skills needed for business.

From learning Microsoft Office to understanding Flash or other Adobe products like PhotosShop, to learning about web design or WordPress, to producing a marketing plan; new courses are constantly added and upgraded to match the most current needs of their students. The best thing about membership at Lynda.com is that it gives you unlimited access to everything in the massive video library. Free mobile apps allow these to be viewed on an iPhone or another type of handheld Internet device. Of course, selecting what you want to learn, when there is such a big library of videos to choose from, can be cumbersome.

So what does it cost? Lynda's pricing scheme is a two-tiered 'all-you-can-eat' approach. The cost for standard membership is $24.99 per month with a significant discount if paid annually. The Premium membership, at this writing, is $34.99 per month, or $359.88 a year, provides more learning tools, including searchable playlists and transcripts. Premium membership also allows downloaded course materials and tools to be used offline, even on an Android device, iPad or iPhone.

Global Knowledge

Global Knowledge is a big international site offering expert IT training. The site has a full catalog of courses in areas of business skills and technical competencies, with many leading to certification.

There are more than a thousand classes available in the Global Knowledge Virtual Classroom. They also provide live online training from expert instructors wherever you are, and you get full access to recordings of your classes for six months, so you can revise what you are learning in them at any time.

Courses are all individually priced. For example, a three-day immersive introduction course, the Agile Boot Camp, costs $1795, and a comprehensive two-day course on adopting cloud computing is $1395. The site does have some special offers and gives discounts when you pay for more than one course at the same time.

SBA Learning Center

Online training from the Small Business Administration web resource includes approximately fifty short courses covering various topics related to marketing, financing, contracting and business management.

The following are just a few examples:

- A guide to patents, trademarks and copyright, which shows you how to protect your intellectual property

- A guide to customer service and its impact on business, which shows you how to implement or improve your customer service

- A guide to cyber-security that identifies cyber threats shows how to guard against them and defines cyber risk management

- Course study is available through worksheets, video presentations, and chat discussions. Certainly the price is right (free), and most of the material is useful to almost any business owner.

Busuu.com

There are 250 language learning units available at this international language website, which offers a quick way to learn enough of a new language to converse at a business meeting or on an overseas trip.

The language units are designed by linguists for easy learning, using images and audio. These are useful when you want to quickly build up a vocabulary for different topics and learn basic grammar in any language.

Video chat is a great feature that allows you to learn how to speak a language and practice having a conversation with native speakers who are international members of the site's online community.

Free apps are available for most devices, so you can learn and practice any language anywhere. The mobile version has fewer distractions than the standard website.

Free and premium versions are available. The free version is offered through support by advertising, which at times can seem intrusive. There is an optional monthly fee if you want to pay for a premium membership that provides access to additional learning materials, podcasts, and language exercises.

The bottom line for most of us is that solutions do exist for picking up that singular necessary skill that may be holding us back from a promotion, new contract or job change. You can, in fact, get technical training for certification or to simply solve that unique problem you may have encountered. Other providers include Udemy and Khan Academy. You can take a language refresher or learn business basics in just a few hours, even get technical certification. You'd be hard-pressed to find a downside for your employer, your career, or yourself.

22

GOOGLE: NOW FOR SOMETHING COMPLETELY DIFFERENT

When companies are small, we think they're cute, hip and spunky. Google was no exception; they had their clever search engine, an innovative way to monetize it and a brave new world of data to collect. Then they became a big company, a gigantic company, a humongous company, and when that happened some of us got a bit suspicious; a bit cynical. While many folks were still focused on government privacy infringements, some of us started to think that maybe companies like Google and Amazon actually knew more about us than the government did!

But this week I had to put that all aside and reflect on the positive impact Google has had on our society. Google founder Larry Page has declared that Google's mission statement was no longer relevant. That the company had outgrown its initial directive "organize the world's information and make it universally accessible and useful."

But was Larry referring to their mission statement or their well-publicized, but since abandoned mantra; "Don't be Evil?" Of course only the future has the answer to that question, but if we're willing to trade any semblance of privacy, Google is prepared to shower the world with some amazing stuff (besides funky glasses) including:

Smart Contact Lenses for Diabetics

With diabetes affecting nearly a third of the world population, Google is developing a contact lens that will help people with diabetes be able to check their glucose level without finger pricking. The contact lens project was announced on 16th January 2014, and will constantly monitor glucose levels by use of tears.

A diabetic will wear a special contact lens that has a wireless chip and a mini glucose sensor. The lens has a pinhole that allows tear fluids to sip into a sensor that measures blood glucose level. A wireless antenna that is thinner than the human hair will be used to relay this information to a controller. Google said they plan to have it viable for public use in 2019.

Wireless Internet Balloons

The Google wireless internet balloon project, also known as project loom is meant to make Internet accessible to 1 billion people. It entails putting floating balloons at the stratosphere. These balloons will be able to travel in areas with no Internet access. People in such areas will be able to connect to the balloon network using special antennas that will be attached to their buildings. The Internet signal bounces from the antenna to the balloon, then back to earth's global internet network. Project balloon began in 2013 and has been tested successfully in New Zealand, California and Brazil.

Ingestible Disease Identification Sensors

To enable early detection of life-threatening diseases like cancer, Google is now working on an ingestible pill that can detect diseases. The aim is to enable medical practitioners to get a full picture of their patients' health and to easily identify diseases that would otherwise take months or even years to manifest.

This pill contains numerous magnetic particles that travel through the bloodstream searching for the malignant cell. These nano-particles transmit their findings to a wearable receiver. According to Google X, these nanoparticles can be coated with antibodies to deal with these malignant cells.

Android@Home

This out of the box innovation that is set to change how we manage our homes. Google intends to automate our homes with an Android operating system. Your home appliances will be connected to the Android system, and you will be able to connect them remotely.

Google envisions a future where the device will be able to order your milk and juice automatically when it detects that they are running low in your fridge. The android@ home project began in 2011 and Google insists that they are still on track and will be soon undertaking real life testing

Driverless Car

Google Car is one of the most publicized Google projects. For a few years now, Google has been testing its driverless car with successful results. The car uses state of the art technology and generates 3D maps and data reports of the driving area. To date, they have tested ten driverless cars and drove over 310,000 miles with not a single major incident. Google has lobbied for legislation to legalize autonomous cars. Four states have legalized driverless cars with Google giving 2017 as a possible release date for these cars to be offered to the public.

Project Wing

Project Wing is a Google drone program that seeks to deliver packages to home conveniently and at the shortest time possible. A drone, which takes off vertically and flies to specified addresses to deliver packages. It delivers the package by winching it down to the ground. Developed secretly since 2012, Google has been carrying out full tests of these delivery drones in Australia, which has relatively few drone laws.

High Attitude Wind Turbines

Most people were unaware of Google's high altitude wind turbine project until it acquired Makani power in May 2013. Makani power is a US company that developed tethered wings with mounted wind turbines. Google plans to generate low-cost power by flying these tethered kites with wind turbines at high altitudes.

A lot of cool stuff from a company with an impressive reputation for innovation and creativity. What can the average business owner take from this seemingly unrealistic array of achievements? First impressions might suggest access to lots of capital or an impressively educated human resource, but deep inside the company, is a willingness to master the latest technologies for business productivity and communication, and maximize their benefits. You don't have to be a $124 billion dollar company to do that.

23

CAN A VERY SMALL BUSINESS
BANK ON THE CLOUD?

I've written four checks in the last four years. I drove to one bank to cancel one brick and mortar bank account. If they had a wall next to every grocery store cashier, I'd be banging my head against it every time someone pulled out their checkbook to write a check. This is 2015, not 1985. While folks might be excused for staying close to their comfort zone, i.e., their favorite checkbook ledger, the same really can't be said for businesses. But surprisingly, while a waning 35% of U.S. consumers still write checks, a whopping 50% of businesses are also paying their bills the old fashion way!

Here in the United States, we pride ourselves on being the center of technology innovation. While it's true, as a nation, we lead the world with some pretty impressive accomplishments. On the other hand, as individual people and small business owners, we're not so quick to adapt, despite our compulsion to glue a smartphone to our hip and stick an earbud in our head. According to Crone Consulting, a business payment strategy consultancy, Europe and other parts of the world, including Latin America, are 20 to 30 years ahead of the US in digital payment adoption.

In fact, in Great Britain, a service called Homelink set up the first home internet banking system in 1983. American banks tried unsuccessfully in the early eighties to mimic this initiative, but the effort went nowhere. It wasn't until 1995 that Wells Fargo added customer account services to its website. If you haven't noticed, our credit cards are inoperable in Europe, and international visitors to the United States often find their cards won't work here. That's because the US financial industry is slow to adopt smart chip technology. Additionally, quite a few small businesses are still mailing transactional agreements, completely unaware that digital signatures are perfectly legal in the US. In fact, Adobe offers an electronic signature service called EchoSign to facilitate online business transactions.

Security or Insecurity

So what exactly stops us from joining the rest of the world in our drive toward the future? Most of us will complain about the lack of security. We all read about the various bank card thieves, the hacks at Target, Home Depot, and others, I've even written about them in earlier chapters. Surely that's enough to make any sane person or responsible business owner take pause. Pause, yes, but screech to a dead stop? No.

According to the last survey administered by the Federal Trade Commission, the fraud most reported wasn't about cyber-attacks, it was about weight-loss products, followed by misleading prize promotions. In fact, more than 10% of the US population were estimated to be recipients of some sort of fraud activity. Surprisingly, less than 41% of these crimes had any connection to the Internet at all, much less personal hacking. To be sure, there is a risk in nearly every human activity we undertake. The question really is, what is the acceptable risk?

So while media and marketing emphasize the potential dangers of using a credit card for web purchases or doing business in the Cloud, millions of companies worldwide have already accepted the reasonable risk of doing business in the digital sky because of the huge advantages that come with participating. American small business owners should consider adjusting their insecurities to the reality of a cloud-based, collaborative business infrastructure. It's here to stay; I'd put my money on it.

24

HOW FAR HAVE WE COME?
A LITTLE WEB HISTORY

In 1993, the Internet was merely a novelty that few people understood and even fewer trusted. Mosaic was the browser of choice and the 130 websites available were simplistic at best. Fast forward to today and Mosaic is long gone, and now you can choose from hundreds of millions of exciting and interactive websites. Let's look at the substantial changes websites have undergone in the past 20 years.

The Basic Designs of 1993

In 1993, Mosaic gave individuals without any technical experience the opportunity to surf the internet. However, most websites were just a text-based page with few, if any, images and had no obvious layout. They were purely informational, a significant contrast to the websites of 2015. Mosaic was followed by:

In June 1993, Cello Browser, the first browser available for the Windows platform, was released. By March 1994, development had ended.

In March 1995, Netscape Navigator 1.1 became the first browser to introduce tables to HTML. This innovation allowed developers to create more complicated layouts and give structure to their designs.

In August 1995, Microsoft climbed into the Web with its first version of Internet Explorer.

In late 1995-1996, the introduction of JavaScript and Flash gave designers the opportunity to use special effects, such as 3D buttons, background images, and splash pages, as well as animation.

In 2001, Drupal 1.0, the Web's first comprehensive content management system (CMS) was released; as of February 2014, over 1,015,000 sites were using Drupal as their CMS.

In May 2003, WordPress 0.7 was introduced as a free and open-source content management system and blogging tool. As of today, it is responsible for more than 60 million websites and is the most popular blogging system used on the Web.

In 2010, Windows Azure, the first Platform as a service (PAAS) was introduced. In 2014, it was renamed Microsoft Azure.

It is interesting to note that although Mosaic wasn't introduced until 1993, online schools were already in existence. The first graduating class from the University of Phoenix graduated in 1991. However, online schools did not become popular until the mid-2000s.

The Table Based Designs of the mid-90s

Table-based designs gave developers the opportunity to design websites that were more structured and creative. Although websites still consisted mainly of text, it was easier to read because it could be formatted in rows and columns. During the mid-90s, dancing GIFs, page hit counters, and animated text also became popular.

Today, the table-based design is no longer popular due to visual inconsistencies, excessive markup, and slow page load times. However, it was an important phase because it caused designers to focus on page structure. For example, an emphasis was placed on where the best location for call-to-actions would be, as well as how it would impact the viewer's experience.

The Late 1990s

In the late 90s, the introduction of Flash created a whole new world of design options that had not previously been possible with HTML including the ability to add rudimentary video and music. During this period, designers directed their efforts toward navigation and structure, as well as focusing on designs that were visually appealing and usable.

Into the 21st Century

Designers now have more creative freedom. It was decided that design could be developed exclusively from content and vice versa. This made websites quicker to load, more flexible, and much easier to maintain. Also, usability became more important than design. Instead of web pages consisting of only links and text, designers started using icons, and pixelation became a more important aspect of web page design. There was also a decrease in brash neon colors and an increase in white space.

Today, web designers know that straightforward navigation, visually highlighted links, and the ability to find exactly what a user is looking for, is key for a great website.

World Wide Web Consortium

Known as W3C, the World Wide Web Consortium was founded in 1994 for the purpose of keeping watch over web coding and designing.

Social Media

There is no denying that social media has had a substantial impact on web culture and internet business. In fact, many large businesses have had to hire staff simply to maintain social networking. They provide the perfect opportunity for positive exposure. In 2015, businesses are likely to begin setting aside larger portions of their marketing budgets for social initiatives. After all, social media is proving to be an effective way to reach customers.

While there is no denying that the written word is the most important aspect of a website, today's developers and designers know how crucial the use of graphics, images, and additional design elements are to creating a contemporary website that catches a user's attention.

25

WILL FRAUD DISSAPEAR
ALONG WITH OUR PRIVACY?

Driving North on Highway 101 in Malibu a while back, I encountered a grisly auto wreck that had happened just moments before. Several cars had been involved; the crash caused several injuries and one fatality. A tragic day for all involved to be sure, but in the aftermath I discovered that the police had appropriated the cell phone of every driver involved in the accident. Apparently, they wanted to determine if any driver was texting or talking at the very moment of the crash.

The details of this particular case are not relevant to this discussion, but the very fact that our connected lives, personal and work-related are being documented in ever increasing detail, in ever more innocuous ways. In this new world, we are always under surveillance. Not only were cell phones given up, but as I drove by, many bystanders were already clicking away furiously, putting moving picture and still, up on YouTube and Facebook before the blood was even dry. No one was going to talk their way out of that one, now that we have the worldwide witness.

In the February 15, 2015, edition of the New York Times, Natasha Singer reports on a woman who, over a period of ten years, received more than fifty-thousand dollars in Medicaid payments. Data scientists were suspicious, and by accessing the LexisNexis Risk Solutions database and the New York state motor vehicle database and other state and city records, they were able to conclude that the woman had in fact committed fraud. The woman and her husband owned three rental properties, had more than a hundred thousand dollars in bank accounts, and an electrical contracting business to boot.

This case and the traffic accident described earlier might lead you to think that 'all eyes are indeed on you' — which at first glance could be cause for some consternation. The reality may be that the impact of big data is very different. In fact, 'all eyes are on all of us – all of the time' may be more apropos, the result of which is that there is a heck of a lot of data to sift through! Already, financial institutions are having a hard time producing actionable intelligence based on current data retrieval methods. Add to that the fact that the Internet, digital transactions, in general, are now processed in real-time. No more five day, float-the-check policy for most businesses or customers. Consequently, whatever fraud protections we employ, they need to be applied at the moment the transaction takes place.

We're living in an age where we aren't sure who the bad guy is. While governments, corporate behemoths, and gargantuan Internet retailers may be picking up every crumb you drop along your digital trail, those evil hackers we've heard so much about recently, who've stolen your credit card numbers along with those of a billion other folk, they've got the same problem: too much data.

26

DON'T WASTE YOUR WEBSITE

If you haven't been living under a rock, you probably have been asked if you have a website. If you're in any way involved in commerce, your answer was probably yes. If you've set up your site correctly, you've also invested in your own domain name, giving just a bit more legitimacy to your online presence. Swell.

The pretty pictures are up, the e-commerce coding is in place, and you've started marketing your site through SEO (Search Engine Optimization) and maybe some Pay-Per-Click (PPC) advertising. If you're like millions of other small and micro business operators, the whole web hosting thing costs you less than ten bucks a month on sites like Hostgator, GreenGeeks, or Godaddy.

A great deal to be sure, but what about the rest of your business? You're probably spending considerably more money on support tools and services, tools that are hidden in the backend of your website, totally under your control, for free.

Most hosting services provide their clients access to their websites via a backend control panel of some sort, the two most popular being Cpanel and Vdesk. You were given a username and password and a separate URL to access this dashboard when you originally signed up for the service.

Let's take GreenGeeks as an example. This company uses the Cpanel dashboard and through its interface, provides a wide range of easily installable software services that you, as a contractor or micro business can use at no extra cost. For example if you need project management, GreenGeeks Softaculous installer provides 20 different free project management choices. Do you feel a bit uneasy using Google Calendar or Outlook for scheduling? Again, Under GreenGeek's Cpanel, five different calendars are available on your website under your complete control. There are nine social network options where you can have your company Facebook. There's a whole lot more than I can touch on here.

The bottom line is; if you're spending money on mailing list software, project management, CRM or commerce services, particularly if they're of the online rental variety, consider exploring the back end of your own shared web hosting service. It can not only save you money but keeps your business under your own control.

27

WHO'S FINDING WORK: DRONES ROBOTS AND SOFTWARE

It should come as no surprise to you that we're not only losing jobs to developing nations but to drones, robots and software as well. Experts estimate that within 20 years, 40% of our jobs will be done by machines. And, tomorrow's man-made employees can do just about anything. From manning the cockpits of ocean-going freighters to major heart surgery to reporting the news, we humans will have to scramble for new gigs or make some pretty hefty stock purchases to stay solvent.

Drones

In December 2013, Amazon announced that they were testing drones as delivery systems. The goal, customers' purchases delivered in 30 minutes or less, certainly sounds appealing. But, have we thought out the ramifications of such a move? The trickle-down effect of actual people who would be put out of work is staggering. Everyone from delivery drivers to the truck manufacturers would become less necessary.

There are reports that drones will eventually take the place of manned police helicopters patrolling the cities. And, military fighter planes are already using drones for some exercises rather than actual people. Again, are we not thinking forward at all? What happens to all of the people who hold these jobs currently? There aren't enough commercial airline pilot jobs to compensate, and let's be honest, commercial airlines will probably not be far behind with unmanned piloting.

Robots

Scientists have created beetle-like robots that work like termites and sense what to do with bricks. They build things much larger than themselves and do so without a foreperson telling them what to do. The inventors expect to see these little machines doing jobs like stacking sandbags to prevent flooding and even building housing structures on other planets. They won't be at the construction site anytime soon, but it will happen.

Google is experimenting with robot assembly lines. These blue-collar manufacturing jobs are currently held by real people. Robots that can run store check-out counters or take tickets at sports and music venues are being tested. We are talking about millions of people being put out of jobs if this technology becomes the norm. Robot vacuums are pretty cool, but I wasn't already paying a maid to do the work.

Software

Evidence of software programs being implemented in almost every career is right in front of us. Servers use computer systems to input customer's orders; librarians use software programs to organize the library's books and mechanics even use computer programs to find car problems. Every single one of these jobs is at risk of having the computer program take over. If your boss only has to buy one software program instead of paying 20 employees, don't you think he's going to do it?

Unmanned, remote controlled workers are the future of employment. We are surrounded by self-checkout grocery lines, Siri giving us directions, Redbox renting us movies and automated answering services when we call almost any office in America. Millions of workers are fighting a losing battle with machines that are simply too fast and too smart to beat. It may be time to invest in tech companies.

28

GENERAL MOTORS, THE IRS AND YOUR BUSINESS
A COMMON THREAD

Back in 2005 when Laura Andres wrote an email to General Motors complaining about a faulty ignition switch, she probably didn't expect that email to be the focus of a federal investigation in 2014, neither did GM Chief Executive Mary Barra. Recently Ms. Barra found herself appearing at a congressional hearing on GM's faulty ignition switches, switches that are linked to 16 deaths and a recall of more than 29 million cars.

In another congressional investigation, the spotlight was on the IRS, somehow two years of email correspondence had gone missing; email that was significant to other pending investigations. Apparently the hard drive where these emails were stored had crashed. Oops.

Two disparate examples of how email became the focal point for serious legal investigations. Two examples of how poor organizational policies came home to roost with senior management causing embarrassment, displaying incompetence and costing millions of dollars in damages.

The one thing your business has in common with GM and the IRS is that it can also be the recipient of legal action. This is America after all, any business big or small can be sued. Virtually every business today employs email, has a website and used networked computers. As Robin Harris writes in his Storage Bits blog recently about the IRS fiasco, "We underfund and undermanage critical IT infrastructures and then wonder why things blow up."

29

WISHFUL THINKING DOESN'T CUT IT

'Out of sight, out of mind' isn't a good strategy for any business. What we're talking about here is your organization's legal requirement to safeguard your business correspondence as outlined by the Federal Rules of Civil Procedure or FRCP. If your business gets sued, you may be required to provide the courts with specific emails and other electronic documents sent or received by individuals in your employ. This process is called eDiscovery. Having a robust IT infrastructure goes without saying, having bulletproof email archiving is essential.

Regulatory compliance is not only an issue for a strictly litigious perspective. Individual companies may have regional or organizational compliance requirements depending on the nature of their enterprise. Governing laws in various states and regions may impose regulatory requirements, often industry specific including the Health Insurance Portability and Accountability Act (HIPAA), the

Federal Information Security Management Act (FISMA) and ISO 27001 among others. If you haven't done so already, your company should do due diligence and review compliance requirements for your business enterprise.

One Solution

Office 365 for Business does a good job of addressing many of these issues, using Microsoft Exchange cloud services like your email backbone; each user has fifty gigabytes of storage for email and other documents. Office 365 also touts eDiscovery, data loss prevention and legal hold among its user controls and admin functions, all extremely helpful when it comes to regulatory compliance. Users can recover deleted emails, import email from legacy Outlook sources and simply drag messages to Exchange online archiving. Microsoft has also established the Office 365 Trust Center in an effort to provide more updated information on transparency, regulatory compliance and security issues.

A legal threat has the potential to turn your growing enterprise in an unmitigated disaster if precautions are not taken, and that includes taking your IT infrastructure and security seriously. While some decisions in the corporate office might be left for another day, shoring up your primary business foundation should not be one of them.

30

THE INTERNET OF THINGS: FUTURE IMPACT

The Internet of Things (IoT) is currently the latest brand package to ignite digital marketing landscape. It, like everything digital before it, is deemed the next big thing by tech experts, with many claiming that it will revolutionize our lives in every way. Is it something new or simply a technical re-gift, assembled in such a way to keep us all excited about digital companies. Here's a quick primer on the Internet of Things.

Put simply, the Internet of Things refers to objects that can be linked and managed via an internet connection. For example, you can currently get smart thermostats that connect to your smartphone, allowing you to control your heating when you're not at home. There are currently around 25 billion gadgets linked to the Internet of Things, and in the next five years it is estimated that this figure will increase to around 50 billion.

The Benefits of IoT

One of the main benefits of the Internet of Things is that it will streamline our lives, making everyday tasks easier. This is already being done to a certain extent; smart homes are being built in which lights, heating, air conditioning and electronics can be controlled remotely via smartphones and tablets. In the future, we can expect the same principle to be used on a larger scale; whole cities could be connected to allow citizens to find empty parking spaces while lanes on freeways or traffic signal patterns could automatically adjust based on the flow of traffic.

The Internet of Things can also give us access to better data that can improve our lives. One example is remote health monitoring devices, which can assess various vitals and even provide alerts to emergency services. For businesses, the Internet of Things could provide better insights about their customers and allow them to provide an improved service. Stores may be able to monitor the movements of their patrons through sensors and deliver bespoke offers to them at the checkout based on their browsing patterns.

What are the future implications of the Internet of Things?

As the Internet of Things grows every day, increasing numbers of people are feeling concerned about privacy and security. If hundreds of objects in our home can be controlled via smartphones and devices, how much personal information can manufacturers or retailers glean from our activities? A survey conducted by the Ponemon Institute and Trend Micro found that 42% of people believe the privacy and security risks outweigh the potential benefits that the Internet of Things could bring. However, as technology develops and more people become accustomed to the applications of the Internet of Things, these attitudes may change.

One thing that many tech experts are particularly excited about is the potential for self-driving vehicles. Not only could this be incredibly convenient for drivers, allowing them to put their commute time to better use, but it could also mean safer roads and an improved flow of traffic in busy areas as vehicles could communicate and monitor one another to prevent accidents and gridlock.

The future of the Internet of Things is certainly bright, and over the next five years we can expect to see more smart gadgets, and more ways in which our lives are made more convenient through this form of technology.

31

TECHNOLOGY FORCAST: MOSTLY CLOUDY

So this is a big deal. I'm writing my first article on Google Docs. It's all happening in the cloud. It used to be the cloud was where you ended up after you passed away. Apparently now it's where I'll have more work from the office waiting for me.

Theoretically with Google Docs, I'm able to put a period right here "." and then turn off my computer, drive to my office. There I would sign on my desktop computer and connect to the Internet and continue writing this article as if I had never left my laptop. Then, even seemingly more amazing (or bewildering depending on your point of view) I can jump on a local bus, pull out my smartphone, access my Google account and even continue writing this very same document right there.

So previously I only needed one computer, I now have three; the one nailed down in my office, the laptop that I could take with me but since I have a smartphone, I can leave it at home and use the phone's tiny keys to do my typing on a bus or while I'm driving my car2go smart car into a wall on the southbound expressway – at which point I'd soon find myself in the cloud where I can finish the article at last. Cool.

ABOUT THE AUTHOR

Gary Paul Bryant started his technology career as a consultant in library software in the late nineteen-eighties. During the formative years of the Web, Mr. Bryant served as a research analyst and later, digital publications editor for a Silicon Valley startup. Over the last fifteen years, he has established himself as a technology analyst, author, and award-winning media creative in music, digital animation, and web design.

***

Did you enjoy reading The Truth About Technology for Very Small Business? If so, I would greatly appreciate your taking the time to write a short review at Amazon.com. If you want to know when my next release is coming out, be sure to sign up to be notified at http://www.garypaulbryant.com

www.ingramcontent.com/pod-product-compliance
Lightning Source LLC
Chambersburg PA
CBHW021437170526
45164CB00001B/279